The Diabetic *foot* Book

The Diabetic *foot* Book

— A GUIDE —
FOR OPTIMIZING FOOT HEALTH

InStride Foot & Ankle Specialists℠

Printed in the United States of America

ISBN Paperback: 978-0-578-47548-6
ISBN eBook: 978-0-578-47548-3

Editing: Proofed to Perfection
Interior and Cover Design: Ghislain Viau

Note from the Authors

This book is for people with diabetes and their loved ones who seek to protect and improve their feet. The book is also designed for health care providers as a resource for patient education and to offer a clinical pathway for the monitoring and care of the diabetic foot. The authors thank Allen Jacobs, DPM and Rob van Brederode, DPM for assistance in the preparation of the manuscript.

Contents

Glossary 1

Chapter 1 — The Diabetic Foot 9

Chapter 2 — Assessment of the Diabetic Foot
      by Jeff Lehrman, DPM 15

Chapter 3 — Diabetic Foot Care Guidelines
      by Jeff Lehrman, DPM 21

Chapter 4 — Exercise for the Diabetic Foot
      by Nicole Caviness, RPT 27

Chapter 5 — Diet for the Diabetic Foot
      by Cherie Hardy, CDE 35

Chapter 6 — Wellness for the Diabetic Foot
      by Cherie Hardy, CDE 39

Chapter 7 — Footwear for the Diabetic Foot
      by Josh White, DPM, C Ped 45

Chapter 8 — Medications for the Diabetic Foot 53

Chapter 9 — Alternative Treatments for the Diabetic Foot
      by Jim Shipley, DPM 57

Chapter 10 — Diabetic Foot Wound Care
      by Thomas Verla, DPM 65

Chapter 11 — Diabetic Foot Surgery 73

Chapter 12 — Diabetic Foot Pathway for Monitoring
 and Care. 77

Appendices 81

   1. Diabetic Foot Care Fundamentals. 83

   2. Prescription for Diabetic Foot Exercises 84

   3. Monthly Log for Foot Exercises. 85

   4. The Plate Method. 86

   5. Weekly Diet Log. 87

   6. Foods to Choose and Foods to Avoid. 88

   7. Glycemic Food Index 90

   8. Wellness, Quality Sleep, and Stress Relief 91

   9. Smoking Cessation 92

  10. Footwear Recommendations. 93

  11. Diabetic Foot Management Pathway. 97

References and Resources 99

About the Authors 101

Glossary

The following terms are used in the book and may not be familiar to the reader. Brief descriptions are supplied in an attempt to be helpful and complete.

ABI (Ankle Brachial Index) is a test that measures circulation to your legs and feet by comparing the blood pressure in your arm to the blood pressure at your ankles. If the blood pressure at your ankle is less than ninety percent of the blood pressure of your arm, you may have peripheral arterial disease (PAD).

ADA (American Diabetes Association) is the organization dedicated to helping people manage, cure, and prevent diabetes mellitus.

ANS (Autonomic Nervous System) is the part of the nervous system responsible for bodily functions not under conscious control, such as the heart beat, the dilation and constriction of blood vessels, and the flight-or-fight response.

Arthropathy is a disease of a joint or joints. People with diabetic neuropathy are at risk for Charcot Arthropathy where the joints of the foot and ankle can break down due to a loss of protective sensation.

BMI (Body Mass Index) is a formula for estimating body fat percentage based on a calculation of the ratio of height to weight. Although not entirely valid for bodybuilders, a BMI of 19 to 24 is considered ideal, over 25 is overweight, and over 30 is obese.

Bunion is a bony bump on the inside border of the foot, at the base of the great toe. Gout frequently affects this area.

CDE (Certified Diabetes Educator) is a health care professional dedicated to teaching people with diabetes how to manage their condition.

Charcot Deformity is a condition where the lack of protective sensation (neuropathy) causes the bones, ligaments, and joints of the foot to break down, leading to fractures, dislocations, and changes in the shape of the foot. In the early stages of Charcot Foot, the foot may become red, swollen, and warm and be mistaken as a foot infection or as gout. Early diagnosis is key for this syndrome in order to prevent long-lasting, significant foot problems.

Claudication is pain caused by a lack of blood flow to the legs, usually during exercise. It starts off as intermittent and may become constant and is an important sign of PAD.

Debridement is the process of removing dead and diseased tissue from wounds and ulcers in order to aid the healing process.

Diabetic Foot Pathway is a protocol for the care and management of the diabetic foot, based on the vascular, neurological, and structural status of the foot as well as the history of prior ulceration or partial amputation of the feet.

DFU (Diabetic Foot Ulcer) is an open sore or wound on the foot of a person with diabetes. This is a preventable complication of diabetes that is often difficult to heal once formed.

Diuretics are medications used to increase the amounts of water and salts expelled from the body as urine.

Equinus is a condition where a person has limited upward mobility of the ankle joint. This can often lead to problems with the toes and forefoot.

Glycemia is the presence of sugar in the bloodstream.

Glycemic Index is a ranking system of foods containing carbohydrates based on how they affect the blood sugar levels. The higher the ranking, the more severe affect the food has on blood sugar levels.

Gout is a form of arthritis caused by excess uric acid in the bloodstream that is typically seen in the foot. Gout can sometimes be mistaken as a foot infection and is more common in people with diabetes.

Hemoglobin A1C is a blood test used to measure blood sugar control over a two- to three-month period. A normal test reading will have a level of less than 5.7; a score between 5.7 and 6.4 indicates pre-diabetes; a level higher than 8.0 indicates poor glucose control and a much higher risk of diabetic foot complications.

Hyperglycemia is when the sugar level in the blood stream is too high, which is a defining characteristic of diabetes.

Hypoglcemia is when the blood sugar level is too low.

Integument is the natural covering of an organism, which includes the skin, hair, and nails of a human.

Libido is a person's overall desire for sexual activity. It can be adversely affected by stress, medications, smoking, alcohol, and a lack of exercise.

MRI (Magnetic Resonance Imaging) is a diagnostic test that can create detailed images of body tissues to evaluate infections, fractures, tumors, and other issues.

Musculoskeletal relates to the muscles and bones of the body together.

Neuropathic Pain is pain caused by damage to the peripheral sensory nerves. There may be complaints of burning, itching, numbness, or shooting pains.

Neuropathy is a range of health problems caused by damage to the peripheral nerves.

Obesity is when a person weighs more than 20 percent above their ideal weight, based on their sex, age, and height. It is also defined as having a BMI of over 30.

Offloading is the process of keeping pressure and weight off of a body surface to aid in healing. Diabetic ulcers on the bottom of the feet require offloading to heal the wound and a TCC is an excellent way to accomplish this.

Osteomyelitis is an infection of a bone, which is a serious and difficult to treat infection.

PAD (Peripheral Arterial Disease) is a narrowing and stiffening of the arteries, which often leads to pain and cramping of the legs (claudication). PAD is the most common form of PVD (peripheral vascular disease).

Pedal means pertaining to the foot or feet.

Plantar means pertaining to the soles of the foot or feet.

Plate Method is a guide for planning meals that promotes eating healthy foods and discourages eating (and drinking) unhealthy foods (i.e., foods that cause a rise in blood sugar).

Protective Footwear Program is a program designed to prevent injury to the feet by wearing appropriate footwear. Diabetics "at risk" are typically placed in this type of program.

Septic Arthritis is an infection within a joint.

Sepsis is when a bacterial infection has entered the bloodstream, which is a very serious event.

Shear is a force acting parallel to the surface of the body. In diabetics with neuropathy, excess shear force can result in tissue damage causing an ulceration.

Statins are a class of drugs used to lower cholesterol levels in the blood. High blood cholesterol levels are associated with an increased risk for the occurrence heart attacks, strokes, and PAD.

Steppage Gait is an abnormal walking pattern seen in people with drop foot or contracture of the Achilles tendons.

Tailor's Bunion is the prominence of the 5th metatarsal bone of the foot, at the base of the 5th toe. It is also called a bunionette.

TBI (Toe Brachial Index) is a diagnostic test comparing the blood pressure of a toe to the blood pressure of the arm. If the toe blood pressure is less than one half of the arm blood pressure, a diagnosis of PAD is likely.

TCC (Total Contact Cast) is a specially applied cast designed to take weight off of the foot in order to heal a diabetic foot ulcer. It works far better than crutches for offloading because the patients can't cheat by walking on the ulcer.

Topical Medications are medicines applied to a body surface as a cream, gel, lotion, foam, or ointment.

Turgor is used in the assessment of the skin of the foot to describe the extent of dehydration or fluid loss.

Ulcer is a defect in the surface of an organ or tissue, often occurring in the feet of people with diabetic foot disease.

Vascular Status is the rating of the circulation provided to the extremities of the body. PAD involves an impaired vascular status that can be hard to detect but is a very important cause of kidney failure, blindness, heart attacks, strokes, and the need for a foot amputation.

Vasodilation is the widening of blood vessels and can be helped by the use of vasodilating medications.

CHAPTER 1

The Diabetic Foot

If you have diabetes, I'm sure you've been told countless times that you should take special care of your feet. However, many diabetics don't understand exactly how diabetes can affect the foot. If you're baffled by the science behind diabetes and foot health, then you've come to the right place for answers. In the following pages, written by medical professionals with intimate understanding about this topic, we'll explain *why* you should take special care of your feet.

How does blood sugar level relate to your feet? This chapter will outline how excess glucose in your blood will greatly increase your chances of developing a foot problem. A key takeaway is that prevention is the best treatment for all diabetic foot problems.

Circulation

It is best for your arteries—the blood vessels carrying blood from your heart to the rest of your body—to be wide and flexible. This allows oxygen and nutrients to be carried to all the cells in your body with optimal ease. However, when there is excess sugar in the bloodstream, changes occur in the linings of the arteries that tend to make them narrower and stiffer over time. Decreased blood flow to the feet is an important cause of other diabetic foot complications, which can lead to pain or amputation. One of the goals of this book is to give you tools to combat the narrowing and stiffening of the arteries in your feet and legs. Keeping your blood sugar under tight control is one of the most important thing you can do to preserve the circulation and health of your feet. Other tools to promote foot and leg circulation will be discussed throughout the following chapters.

Sensory Nerves

Your sensory nerves carry information from the outside world to your brain. Excess sugar in the body can lead to these nerves becoming less functional over time. For diabetics, this problem usually shows up first in the toes and feet. Initial symptoms may include tingling of the toes, burning or shooting foot pain, or an itching and "buzzing" sensation in the feet. If the blood sugar remains high over time, permanent numbness, stiffness, or the complete loss of feeling may occur in the feet. Loss of protective sensation to the feet is a major cause of foot ulceration and amputation. As a diabetic, you should know the sensory nerve status of your feet, since loss of sensation can lead to foot misery.

Motor Nerves

Motor nerves transmit impulses from the central nervous system to your muscles to cause movement. The motor nerves are thicker than sensory nerves, so damage to motor nerves from excess blood sugar usually shows up after sensory nerve damage has already occurred. Motor neuropathy can lead to muscle weakness, balance issues, and joint contractures in the feet as well as loss of reflexes.

Autonomic Nerves

The Autonomic Nervous System (ANS) is the set of nerves that control the "automatic" adjustments your body makes to changing conditions. The ANS maintains the balance of body functions through the parasympathetic and sympathetic nerves. Examples of autonomic nerve function are when the heart rate increases and the pupils of the eyes widen during times of stress. Another example is when the sweat glands release more fluid when the body temperature rises. Autonomic nerve damage in the feet may cause symptoms and signs such as cold feet, brittle nails, hair loss, and excess skin dryness. Autonomic nerve damage can also affect the micro-circulation of the feet, leading to slower wound healing. If you notice a wound isn't healing as quickly as it should, this could be a sign of a bigger problem.

The autonomic nerves are smaller and have thinner coatings than the sensory and motor nerves and thus are prone to early damage from excess sugar in the body. In addition, autonomic nerve damage can cause symptoms such as light-headedness, night sweats, and problems with digestion, urination, and sexual function. Always mention any new physical symptoms you experience to your health care providers.

Diabetic Foot Skin and Nails

The skin and nails of your feet may be affected by diabetes when the circulation and nerve functions of your feet are damaged by too much sugar in the bloodstream. The skin will tend to become less supple and prone to corn and callus formation. The nails will tend to become thicker and change shape. Loss of protective sensation can lead to the corns and calluses becoming wounds, and the nails becoming infected with fungus or bacteria. Blisters may occur from excess pressure to areas on your feet such as between the toes and along the sides of the forefoot (the front of the foot). Seek urgent medical attention if you have a wound on the bottom of your foot, or a cut that won't heal or is infected on another part of your foot.

Diabetic Foot Bones and Joints

Excess blood sugar can lead to decreased bone strength over time. People with diabetes will also tend to heal fractures slower than people with normal blood sugar. If diabetic foot disease leads to sensory and motor neuropathy, a condition called "hammertoes"—a deformity that causes one's toes to curl or bend downward—may develop over time. Loss of padding and protective feeling on the bottoms of the feet may cause the metatarsal bones to protrude as "pressure points," causing foot ulcers that are notoriously hard to heal. If the neuropathy becomes severe enough, excess pressure on the bones and joints of the feet may cause the bones to break and the joints to dislocate. This syndrome, known as "Charcot Foot," typically starts with the development of a warm, swollen, inflamed mid-foot, rear-foot, or ankle that may progress into a very flat or otherwise deformed foot and ankle. This very serious complication of diabetes is a primary reason why people with diabetic neuropathy need to wear protective footwear and report any swelling, redness, or changes in shape of the foot to their doctor immediately.

Diabetic Immune System

Our bodies are best able to fight infections when our blood sugars are kept under control. When there is elevated sugar in the bloodstream, the sugar partially disables the white blood cells, which are vital to our immune defenses. As a result, people with elevated blood sugar are more susceptible to developing foot infections and take longer to recover from them.

Diabetic Co-Factors

Elevated sugar in the bloodstream will often cause damage over time to the small blood vessels in the kidneys. The kidneys produce proteins required by the body for healing. As a result, diabetics with decreased kidney (or renal) function will experience foot wounds that are stubborn to heal.

Elevated sugar in the bloodstream also tends to cause damage to the small blood vessels in the eye, resulting in impaired vision. Diabetics with impaired vision will be at a disadvantage in detecting their own foot problems.

People with high blood glucose levels can become "sick and tired of being sick and tired." Having a chronic disease can lead to feelings of depression, anxiety, and stress in many people. Increased stress and anxiety can lead to increased blood sugar in people with diabetes which, sadly, leads to even more stress and anxiety. It is impossible not to get tired of having diabetes, eventually.[1] For help with this challenge, please refer to Chapter 6.

---

1 "Diabetes Distress," Gebel, Erika, *Diabetes Forecast*, June, 2013.

CHAPTER 2

Assessment of the Diabetic Foot

Among patients with diabetes, foot-related diabetic complications are the most common reason for hospitalization. There are often tremendous financial costs associated with diabetic foot disease. It is essential that we try to prevent diabetic foot complications before they occur, rather than try to treat them after they have already developed. One of the best weapons we have in preventing diabetic foot complications is a good, thorough physical exam accompanied by appropriate imaging modalities. A thorough exam includes evaluating the vascular, dermatologic, musculoskeletal, and neurologic status of the feet. Imaging involves both traditional and advanced technologies that provide more information about both the musculoskeletal and vascular status of the feet.

Vascular Status

The evaluation of the vascular status of the foot begins with a visual inspection. Visualizing skin turgor (elasticity), skin texture, skin color, hair growth, and skin pigmentation can provide clues about the underlying vascular status. Thin skin, pale skin, discolored skin, and decreased hair growth are all signs of diminished circulation. Assessment for the presence or absence of edema (swelling due to excess fluid in skin tissues) as well as the presence or absence of varicosities (varicose veins) and telangiectasias (spider veins) is useful as well. Following visualization, an attempt to palpate the pedal pulses should be made, accompanied by evaluation of capillary refill time and skin temperature. A Doppler ultrasonic probe may also be utilized to attempt to listen to the arterial flow. There are several situations which warrant even more advanced evaluation of vascular status. These include:

a. Non-palpable pedal pulses
b. Palpable pedal pulses in the presence of any diabetic-related pedal pathology
c. Any diabetic over age 50
d. Patients younger than age 50 with multiple risk factors for peripheral arterial disease

You may have your vascular status further evaluated by more advanced techniques including Ankle Brachial Indexing (ABI), Toe Brachial Indexing (TBI), and other more sophisticated tests when indicated.

Neurological Status

Peripheral neuropathy is the leading cause of many devastating diabetic foot complications, so early detection is essential. There are multiple ways to assess a patient's neurologic status. Fortunately, these are mostly inexpensive and simple tests. These include

10-gram monofilament, pinprick sensation, ankle reflexes, tuning fork test, and vibration perception threshold. Sensory loss detected with the monofilament or pinprick sensation methods is associated with a significantly increased risk of ulceration, as is an absence of ankle reflexes. The tuning fork test provides a less exact assessment of vibratory sensation, whereas vibration perception threshold testing provides a quantitative assessment of vibratory sensation.

Integumentary Exam

The integumentary system of the foot is comprised of the pedal skin, hair, and nails. The skin of diabetic patients can provide many clues about underlying pathology. This exam should begin with an overall inspection of all skin surfaces of the feet, including the toenails, looking for any wounds, ulcers, defects, abnormal growths, areas of discoloration, callus formation, and abnormal turgor or texture. One must not forget to conduct this exam interdigitally, as pathology between the toes is sometimes missed with incomplete examinations. Any abnormal areas detected on this overall inspection warrant more thorough investigation. Any defects, ulcers, or wounds should be measured and photographed with all of their characteristics documented.

Musculoskeletal Exam

Similar to the integumentary exam, the musculoskeletal exam should begin with an overall inspection. This should include an assessment of the alignment and symmetry of both lower extremities. One is also looking for any gross deformities. These can include contracted toes, bunions, tailor bunions, arch abnormalities, and other conditions. A collapse of the arch of the foot may raise concern for Charcot arthropathy, more commonly known as Charcot foot syndrome. Any musculoskeletal aberration that leads to abnormally prominent bone can create an area of friction and risk for ulceration. Another important component of the musculoskeletal exam is muscle strength testing of the major muscle groups, including the anterior and posterior component muscles. Range of motion testing of all the major joints of the foot and ankle should be performed. Equinus of the ankle joint has a role in many of the complications of diabetic foot disease. The presence or absence of pain with both muscle strength and range of motion testing should be noted. Measurement of both lower extremities helps to evaluate for any potential limb length discrepancy.

Gait Analysis

Much information can be gleaned from a gait analysis performed by a physician with a well-trained eye. Gait abnormalities can provide clues regarding underlying neurologic and musculoskeletal problems, and also help pinpoint sites at high risk for ulceration. A steppage gait or drop foot can be a sign of underlying neurologic problems. Other gait abnormalities can be a manifestation of muscular imbalance, limb length discrepancy, muscle weakness, and other musculoskeletal pathology. Gait analysis may be performed by watching a patient walk or by using more advanced sensor-based technology.

Footwear

Evaluating the footwear of a diabetic patient is of critical importance. With the high risk of pedal ulceration among diabetics, it is important that shoes fit well, with no friction, and provide adequate support. Of particular interest are the height of the toe box, the depth of the heel, materials of the shoe, and appropriate fit. Some diabetics may qualify for custom footwear, specially made to fit and protect their feet. It is essential that diabetics that don't wear custom footwear select shoes that fit well and provide adequate protection.

Radiography

X-rays provide insight regarding not only the bony structure of the foot but also the alignment of those bones. All diabetics do not require baseline x-rays as a matter of course. However, x-rays can be very useful when underlying bony pathology is present or suspected. An example is when a diabetic patient presents with redness, heat, and/or swelling of their entire foot or part of their foot. Especially if this involves a joint, differential diagnoses may include osteomyelitis, Charcot arthropathy, gout, and septic arthritis. With the wide range of different treatment options for these different pathologies, it is important to establish a diagnosis. Radiography is usually inexpensive and readily available and can quickly provide much information that helps narrow down these differential diagnoses.

Charcot arthropathy can have devastating effects on not only the foot, but also the patient's life. The key to Charcot is catching it early. Early identification and intervention in the form of immobilization and offloading can blunt or eliminate the potentially devastating effects of Charcot. While more advanced imaging is available, oftentimes x-ray alone allows an early diagnosis of Charcot.

Other Studies

Radiography is just one imaging modality used to evaluate the diabetic foot below the skin surface. Other imaging studies may be employed as well. Oftentimes clinicians are presented with the challenge of differentiating osteomyelitis from Charcot. Plain film radiography is often very useful in helping make this differentiation but sometimes more advanced techniques are needed. Both bone biopsy and synovial biopsy are invasive procedures that can help make this differentiation. Imaging options include MRI, different types of bone scans, CT scan, and others. Of these, MRI offers the highest combination of sensitivity and specificity in differentiating osteomyelitis from Charcot arthropathy.

CHAPTER 3

Foot Care Guidelines

According to an old proverb, an ounce of prevention is worth a pound of cure. Heeding that advice is especially worthwhile with regard to diabetic foot complications, which are often costly and difficult to treat. People with diabetes often experience neuropathy, and so are unable to sense many things that non-diabetic people can. Therefore, diabetic patients often cannot rely upon sensing or feeling a problem as it develops. That's where the ounce of prevention comes in. Patients with diabetes can employ simple self-assessment techniques on their own—or with the help of a loved one or friend—to identify an area of concern and seek treatment before it blossoms into a true problem.

Self-Care Checklist

The following 12 "ounces of prevention" are recommended for general foot health, and for early detection of potential foot problems:

1. **Inspect your feet.** Look at the bottoms (plantar surfaces) of your feet every night, checking for any areas of discoloration,

as well as any cracks, openings, or bleeding. If any these warning signs are present, see a podiatrist as soon as possible, as a chronic, limb-threatening diabetic foot ulcer can develop very quickly. If you have difficulty seeing the bottoms of your feet, or positioning your feet for proper inspection is a problem, a mirror may be used. Holding the foot up to a standing mirror or employing a hand-held mirror with an extending arm both allow excellent visualization of the plantar aspect of the feet.

2. **Never walk barefoot.** Anywhere. *Ever!* The neuropathy that often accompanies diabetes can lead to numbness on the plantar surfaces of the feet. Patients may not even know this is present. The numbness can involve a large or small area of the foot. The danger lies in stepping on something with a surface of the foot that is numb. When this occurs, the patient may not feel it. Diabetic patients are often surprised to learn they have had a staple or an earring backing or an insulin needle in their foot for days or weeks. In a typical occurrence, a diabetic patient steps on something sharp, causing a break in the skin on the bottom of their foot that they cannot feel. As a result, they fail to seek medical attention; a small sore may turn into an infection, requiring amputation in a worst-case scenario. Simply wearing house shoes or bedroom slippers with a thick sole around the house can prevent these dire consequences. Wouldn't you rather have an insulin needle stuck in the sole of your shoe, rather than your foot? Of course you would!

3. **Keep feet clean and dry.** Feet should be washed with soap and water at least once a day. After washing, they should be dried well.

A wet foot placed into a sock and shoe can lead to breakdown of the skin and other problems.

4. **Soak your feet?** Some diabetic patients enjoy soaking their feet, but care should be exercised. The danger with diabetics is that their neuropathy may prevent them from detecting the actual temperature of the water. People with diabetes have sustained burns on their feet by soaking them in water they didn't realize was scalding hot. Soaking may or may not be advised for patients with diabetes depending on their risk level, degree of neuropathy, and other factors. For those than can enjoy the benefits of soaking their feet, it is a good idea to test the water temperature with a finger before placing a foot in the water.

5. **Moisturize!** Patients with diabetes may have compromised hydration to their legs and feet. Skin that is too dry can form fissures or cracks. These openings can serve as a portal through which bacteria enter. Recommendations vary depending on the climate and the individual patient, but moisturizing lotion should generally be applied to the lower legs and feet twice a day. Care should be taken to not apply moisturizing lotion between the toes, as these areas are normally moist enough, and adding more moisture can lead to breakdown of the skin.

6. **See a podiatrist!** All diabetic patients should have an initial evaluation with a podiatrist. Podiatrists provide thorough counseling to diabetic patients regarding foot care and preventative measures. They also perform a complete lower extremity exam and are skilled in detecting early signs of pathology. After this initial evaluation, regular exams should be followed, with

multiple factors, including the risk level of the patient, determining frequency.

7. **Nail and callus care.** At this initial podiatrist visit, a discussion should be had about the safety of toenail and callus care. In many cases, the podiatrist may inform the patient that it is not safe for them to attempt to cut their own toenails. Many diabetic patients have this type of risky foot care performed by a podiatrist on a regular basis. If a diabetic patient attempts to cut their own toenails, it is important that they take care to never cut their own skin and avoid causing any bleeding. If you have impaired sensation or impaired circulation to your feet, never do your own foot care.

8. **Inspect the insides of shoes before donning.** The neuropathy that often accompanies diabetes may not allow someone affected to feel an object in their shoe when putting it on. Patients with diabetic neuropathy have worn a shoe all day that had something in it, had that object rubbing on their skin and not felt it, and developed an ulcer that, regrettably, necessitated amputation. Looking in a shoe or feeling in it with a hand can help to prevent this highly preventable outcome.

9. **Avoid tobacco use.** Many of the same complications that diabetes can cause are also caused by tobacco use. Just like diabetes, tobacco use can have a negative impact on the circulation, nerve function, skin integrity, and healing capacity of the tissues of the feet. Diabetes alone creates enough of a risk for pedal pathology. Adding tobacco significantly increases that risk.

10. **Blood sugar control.** Many of the diabetic foot complications discussed in this book can be prevented with excellent blood sugar control. The circulatory, neurologic, dermatologic, and orthopedic complications of diabetes that can impact the feet are all much more likely to happen when glucose—a simple sugar in the blood the human body needs for energy—is poorly controlled. Careful attention to diet and taking prescribed medications as directed are key to keeping glucose well controlled. The Hemoglobin A1C test is a blood test that measures your sugar control over the preceding three months. A score of over 7.0 typically needs improvement. You should know your Hg A1c score and your target Hg A1c score.

11. **Stay active!** Activity, combined with excellent glycemic control, can slow or prevent the development of some of the pedal complications diabetic patients most often experience. Safe and appropriate levels of activity vary according to the individual. Some may walk on an athletic track daily, while others may benefit from just going up and down the stairs of their home several times a day. For others, the most appropriate exercise may be seated leg lifts or knee bends. A professional can recommend appropriate types, frequency, and intensity of exercise, depending on the patient.

12. **Know your Diabetic Foot Class:**
   1. No Significant Issue
   2. Impaired Nerve Function
   3. Impaired Blood Flow to the Feet (PAD)
   4. Structural Deformity of the Feet
   5. Prior Foot Ulcer and/or Amputation—
      this category requires extra special attention

CHAPTER 4

Diabetic Foot Exercise

Precautions

Regular exercise is important for people with diabetes to assist with controlling blood sugar levels and improving vascular health. While most exercises are generally safe, always consult your physician before beginning an exercise program and observe the following precautions.

- **Blood Sugar Levels**—Always check blood sugar levels prior to and after exercise. Do not begin exercising if blood sugar levels are less than 100mg/dl prior to exercise. If you are performing high intensity exercises for long periods lasting 30-60 minutes, be sure to have a carbohydrate snack or glucose tablets with you.

- **Heart Conditions**—If you have a heart condition, please consult your doctor before beginning any exercise program.

Strenuous exercise and some strengthening exercises may need to be avoided.

- **Recent Surgery**—If you have had any recent surgeries, please consult with your surgeon. You may have weight-bearing and range of motion exercise restrictions.

- **Increased Pain**- All exercise should be performed slowly, in a pain-free range of motion. It is normal to feel some muscle soreness afterwards but do not ignore significant or increased pain. Consult with your health care provider to modify your exercise activities.

- **Footwear**—Proper footwear is very important when exercising. Shoes should fit properly with no areas of pain or pressure. Your podiatrist can recommend proper shoes for you.

- **Foot Ulcers/breakdown**—Inspect your feet daily for pressures sores and redness. If you see any signs of skin breakdown, you may need to avoid weight-bearing exercises so that further complications do not develop.

Walking

Walking is one of the most important and accessible forms of exercise for diabetic patients. Walking will help assist in glucose control, improved cardiovascular health, and weight control. When walking alone, always wear a diabetic ID bracelet and carry glucose pills or carbohydrate snacks. Begin walking 10 min/day, increasing 1-2 minutes/day until you can tolerate a 30-60-minute walk at least 4-5x/week. Begin walking on flat surfaces, gradually adding hills as tolerated. Keep a comfortable pace and wear proper shoes. If you have difficulty with motivation, using a pedometer is a great way to track your distance and keep yourself accountable. Try to walk at least 10,000 steps/day. If you do not have a walking partner and don't feel comfortable walking alone on the street or in a park, mall walking is a good alternative.

Stretching and Range of Motion

Stretching helps reduce stress, improve flexibility and posture, and lowers your chance of injury. Stretching should be included in your daily exercise program. In order to get the benefits of stretching, hold each stretch at least 30 seconds. Hold the stretch—do not bounce or waggle your stretches. It is recommended that you finish your workouts with stretching to reduce muscle soreness and prevent injury. Range of motion exercises help improve joint function. Joint stiffness is a common problem for people with diabetes due to impaired circulation. These exercises will help improve mobility. Try to perform range of motion exercises daily.

Figure 1: *Ankle Pumps — Point and flex your foot in a pain-free range of motion. Do 20 to 30 reps with each foot.*

Then try to circle the foot clockwise and counterclockwise. Do 20 to 30 reps with each foot.

Figure 2: *Marble Pickup — Place marbles on the floor and pick them up with your toes. Try to pick up 20 marbles with each foot.*

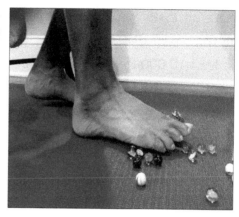

Figure 3: *Belt Stretch — Place a belt or a towel around the front of your foot and flex the foot up and down. Hold each direction for 20 seconds and do 3 reps with each foot.*

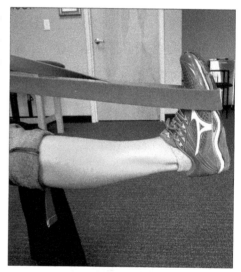

Strengthening

Strengthening exercises make your muscles stronger and can reduce your chances of injury. Strengthening can also reduce neuropathic pain and help control blood sugar levels. Do the following exercises at least 3 to 5 times per week. Do them slowly in a controlled range of motion.

Figure 4: *Marching — Stand in front of a chair or a counter. Lift one leg and then the other, like you are marching in place. Do 20 to 30 reps with each foot.*

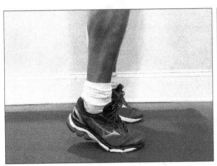 

Figure 5: *Heel and Toe Raises — Stand in front of a chair or a counter. Lift up on your toes and then your heels. Do 20 to 30 reps with each foot.*

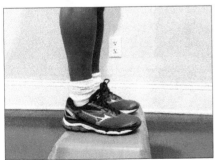 

Figure 6: *Step Downs — Stand with both feet on a small step. Step back with one leg and then bring the foot back onto the step. Switch feet back and forth for a total of 20 reps for each foot.*

Balance

Peripheral neuropathy can leave your muscles and joints feeling stiff and cause you to lack sensation in your feet. This greatly increases your risk of falls. Balance exercise can help improve strength and stability, decreasing the likelihood of a fall.

Figure 7: *Single Leg Stance – Stand in front of a chair or a counter. Stand on one leg for as long as you are able. Try to do this for 20 to 30 seconds. Do 3 to 5 reps for each leg. Try this exercise with your eyes closed for extra credit!*

Figure 8: *Toe Taps – Tap your right foot on a small step in front of you and then tap your left foot on the step. Repeat 20 times for each foot.*

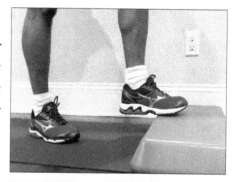

Figure 9: *Tandem Stand – Stand in front of a counter or a chair. Try to balance and stand with one foot in front of the other for as long as you are able. Hold for 20 to 30 seconds. Do 3 reps for each foot.*

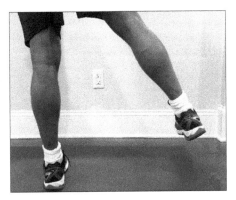

Figure 10: *Standing Leg Lifts - Stand in front of a counter or a chair. Lift one leg out to the side. Hold for 2 to 3 seconds. Do 20 to 30 reps with each leg.*

General Health

Research has proven that people who exercise regularly have a significant reduction in chronic disease. Consistent exercise is a key to staying healthy. Your goal is to try to incorporate exercises into your daily routine. Ultimately, your health is largely up to you!

Weight Loss

If you suffer from Type 2 diabetes and are overweight, weight loss can lower your blood glucose levels and help prevent or reduce the severity of many of the complications associated with the disease. Weight loss can also reduce your blood pressure and cholesterol levels, and may lead to a reduction in the number of medications you need to take. Exercise is also helpful in managing stress, increasing your libido, and promoting physical and mental well-being. Exercise can help you achieve all of these things! Be consistent and you will gradually see results.

CHAPTER 5

Nutrition for the Diabetic Foot

There is no "one size fits all" diet for people with diabetes. The following key principles can help you control your blood sugar and improve your overall health:

a. Be consistent with mealtimes
b. Use portion control
c. Take your time while eating
d. Stop eating when you are full
e. Avoid drinks containing sugar
f. Read labels while shopping
g. Choose fresh food (fruits and vegetables)
h. Put non-starchy vegetables on your plate first
i. Limit sauces and dressings on your food
j. Plan ahead when eating away from home

Foods to Eat

- Green, leafy, and non-starchy vegetables
- Whole grains
- Lean meats – cut off the fat
- Fresh fruits
- Healthy fats
- Beverages without sugar
- Foods rich in fiber

Foods to Avoid

- Drinks containing sugar
- Fried foods
- Processed foods (foods from a box or a can)
- Salty foods
- Jumbo-sized drinks
- Supersized portions
- Second helpings

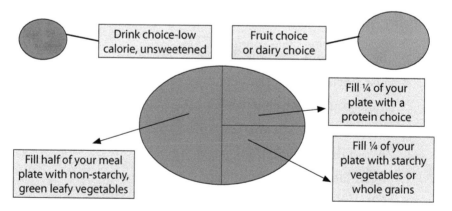

Figure 1: *The Plate Method – You should cover half your plate with leafy vegetables at the start of every meal and put lean protein and other vegetables and grains on the other half of the plate.*

Weight Loss Programs – Even a slight reduction in your body weight can improve blood sugar control and decrease risk of diabetic complications. Weight loss programs focus on the following:

- Understanding eating patterns and triggers
- Focus on portion control
- Increase your physical activity
- Set realistic weight loss goals
- Focus on long-term changes in eating patterns

The Glycemic Index – This is a commonly used measure of the impact of certain foods on blood sugar levels. The higher the Glycemic Index score, the more that food will tend to raise your blood sugar. A list of common foods with a Gylcemic Index can be found in Appendix 6. Key points to consider include:

There are three categories to the Index – Low (less than 55), Medium (56 to 69, and High (70 or more).

Foods that do not contain sugar are not part of the Index.

The ripeness of fruit (riper has more sugar) and the type of cooking method can impact the Glycemic Index's effect on blood sugar.

CHAPTER 6

Wellness for the
Diabetic Foot

Your lifestyle plays a very important role in managing your diabetes and in promoting good foot health. The following are key principles in maintaining overall wellness through positive habits and a healthy lifestyle:

Sugar Monitoring

It is important to monitor your blood sugar as recommended by your doctors.

You should know what your Hemoglobin A1c Level is – this is a measure of your average blood sugar over the last 3 months.

Talk to your doctor about what Hemoglobin A1c level you should aim for. For many people, less than 7.0 is a good goal in order to avoid foot problems.

- Keep a record of your blood sugar level and note when it rises.
- Take this record with you to your health care appointments.
- Your Hg A1C should be checked at least once a year if you are in good control.
- If you have poor glycemic control, testing of your Hg A1C should be done every three months until you reach your target level.
- To help you reach your Hg A1C target, your physician will prescribe strategies personalized to your individual needs; this regimen may include changing medications and developing new habits.

Sleep

Lack of sleep can impact your overall health. If you are not sleeping well, you may notice that it is difficult to maintain your blood sugars. A change in your sleep habits could also be a sign that you are depressed. Depression can lead to other complications and is common when dealing with chronic illness. You should share any concerns that you have about sleep patterns and/or developing depression with your doctor or counselor as soon as possible.

- Tips to improve sleep include:
    - Go to bed and get up on a consistent schedule, even on weekends.
    - Keep your sleep environment dark and free of electronic devices, including televisions.
    - Do not look at electronic devices before bed.
    - Maintain the room temperature at a level comfortable for you.

- ○ Exercise daily.
- ○ Avoid daytime napping.
- ○ Avoid caffeine before bed.
- ○ Limit or abstain from alcohol.
- ○ If you are on medications that interrupt sleep, such as diuretics (water pills), talk to your care team about changing the timing of those medications.
- ○ Shift workers may benefit from blackout curtains.

Smoking

Smoking causes harm to your overall health. There are many benefits to quitting smoking. Some of those benefits are immediate. Your vital signs, such as your blood pressure and pulse, are positively impacted within an hour of quitting. When you stop smoking, blood flow increases throughout your body, including to your feet. If you have a wound on your foot, quitting smoking will significantly promote healing.

Avoiding smoking will also help prevent long-term issues. Your care team will discuss your smoking status during your healthcare visits. If you are thinking about quitting smoking, your care team can provide resources to help you.

There are several stages of readiness when it comes to behavior changes, such as smoking cessation. It is vitally important that you are *committed* to the behavior change you are seeking. Quitting smoking requires your strong desire and commitment to be successful. Keep in mind, relapses and setbacks can happen. If they do, don't get discouraged. Reevaluate your goals with your care team and stay positive! Having support from those around you will help you succeed.

When you decide to stop smoking, there are several important things you should do:

- Set a firm quit date and stick to it.
- Let your family, friends, and coworkers know that you are quitting.
- Develop a plan for times when you may struggle. Write down when you normally smoke, including any associated activities, and prepare accordingly.
- Get rid of anything smoking-related in your home, your workplace, and even your car.
- Talk to your doctor about medications that can help you quit.
- Avoid alcohol, stress triggers, and being alone with other smokers.
- Ask for help if you need it!

Alcohol

Alcohol does not have to be eliminated from your diet when you have diabetes. However, it is important to realize the impact it can have. If you choose to drink alcohol, doctors recommend no more than two drinks per day for men and one per day for women. Alcohol can worsen diabetes complications and lower blood sugar levels when used with certain medications. Alcohol can also increase the symptoms of peripheral neuropathy. The sugar content in alcohol should be considered when planning meals. If overlooked, your meal may contain too many sugar calories, playing havoc with controlling your blood sugar.

Stress Reduction

Stress can increase your blood sugar levels. To reduce stress, it is vitally important to: recognize the personal stress triggers in your life; work on how you respond to them; and identify ways to limit these causes. Having a chronic illness itself can cause stress due to the demands of daily management. Always remember, no one can eliminate stress; the goal is to manage it.

The following habits can help you manage stress:
- Join a support group.
- Exercise daily (see Chapter 4 for ideas).
- Meditate and practice deep breathing daily.
- Find a hobby that you enjoy.
- Practice positive thinking – always look for the good!
- Celebrate small improvements and successes when they happen.
- Get restful sleep.
- Avoid excessive caffeine and alcohol consumption.

CHAPTER 7

Diabetic Footwear

Proper footwear is an important part of decreasing the chance that people with diabetes will develop foot problems.

If your diabetes is complicated by the loss of protective sensation in your feet, or by decreased blood flow to your feet, your risk of foot problems and ulceration is greatly increased. You are therefore classified as "at risk" for foot problems and are likely to require protective shoes. You should know if your feet are considered "at risk"—ask your podiatrist or your primary care doctor if you are not sure.

Unfortunately, most "at-risk" people who get protective shoes wear them far less than they should. Your compliance with wearing therapeutic footwear generally requires the combined efforts of family members, caregivers, and health care providers. When they encourage you to always wear the prescribed shoes, and to inspect your feet on a daily basis for early signs of trouble, listen to them! They want you to put your best foot forward, so to speak.

Shoe Shape and Size

Feet come in different shapes and sizes, and so do shoes. Some feet are thick and broad and muscular; some feet are lean and bony. Some feet have high arches; some have low arches. Sometimes the shape of one foot is very different from the shape of the other. Simply stated, the shape of your shoes should match the shape of your feet.

Proper shoe sizing is very important. Shoes that are too short or narrow can put too much pressure on the toes or the sides of your feet. Shoes that are too loose can cause friction and rubbing of the feet, resulting in blisters or wounds. Be very careful when selecting shoes to ensure that they fit properly.

Shoe Materials / Design

Breathability of the shoe is important, whether the shoe is made of leather or synthetic components. Internal seams should not pass directly over any bony prominences—that is, projections or bumps that may be a natural enlargement of a bone, or an extra bone. The shoe should bend most easily at the widest part of the forefoot, the same as where the foot bends when walking. A closed toe and heel are recommended for the footwear to fit most securely and to best protect the feet. Firmness around the heel will help to keep the foot balanced and supported. Slip-on shoe styles should be avoided as they lack adjustability; Velcro closures may improve ease of use if you have difficulty tying laces.

Shoe features that can improve stability and increase balance include: (a) heel height that is no more than half an inch higher than the forefoot, (b) comfortable and lightweight, (c) good side-to-side support and arch support, and (d) non-slip soles. Shoes that have worn out and have lost stability and support, or have gotten so dirty they are no longer hygienic, should be replaced to prevent problems.

Shoe Insoles

Shoes with removable insoles are highly recommended. Increased support, cushioning, and friction (pressure) reduction can be provided by replacing the insoles that comes with the shoes with insoles specially designed to meet the needs of your diabetic feet. When extra protection and accommodation is needed for high-risk feet, custom insoles can be made by taking a foam impression or digital image of the feet.

Typically, insoles for people with diabetes are designed with a firm bottom layer that provides good arch support and balance. The top layer of the insert is designed to be soft and to reduce the friction between the foot and the supporting surface. Because soft cushioning is associated with a lack of durability, protective shoe inserts should be replaced every few months.

When there are bony prominences on the bottoms or sides of the feet, it is important that they be noted by the technician and accommodated by the insoles, whether by heat molding prefabricated devices at the time of fitting, or by capturing the prominence with the custom mold. The inserts will then have a depression that will decrease pressure on the bony area and transfer weight to the surrounding area.

What Makes for a Good Shoe Fit?

The best way to ensure your feet are properly fitted is by working with an experienced shoe-fitting specialist. When properly fitted, your shoes should not create any pressure on the toes, the tops, or the sides of your feet. They also should not be so roomy as to allow the foot to slide up and down or back and forth within the shoe, even slightly.

Proper shoe fitting entails selecting the correct shoe to match the shape of the foot, as well as the correct length and width. The shoes must also be sized to accommodate the inserts and socks that will be worn. The shoes should also be in a style that suits your taste and you will want to wear. After all, these protective shoes are intended to be worn at all times, not saved for special occasions.

A good shoe fit will also have approximately ¾ of an inch between the end of the longest toe and the end of the shoe. The widest part of the shoe should fit at the widest part of the foot. It's not uncommon for one foot to be slightly larger than the other. Shoe fit can be improved by adding a spacer along the inside of the back of the shoe for a smaller foot.

Custom Shoes

If "off-the-shelf" shoes can't accommodate your foot shape, custom shoes are an option. Custom shoes are made from molds of the feet and thus conform to their unique aspects. They are especially advantageous when the feet are of different sizes and shapes. This commonly occurs with Charcot deformity whereby the foot bones and joints collapse into a deformed fixed position. Custom shoes can incorporate such therapeutic features as lifts when one leg is shorter than the other, partial foot fillers when part of the foot is absent, and bracing when additional support is needed. Once custom shoes are made, the forms on which they were constructed can be saved to make it easier to make subsequent pairs and to improve the fit each time.

Footwear Recommendations for All People with Diabetes

- Understand the importance of proper shoes that fit correctly in maintaining normal activities and an active lifestyle.

- Always wear socks to reduce shear and friction to your skin.

- Ensure that your relatives and caregivers understand the importance of wearing appropriate shoes and help you with your choices.

Footwear Recommendations for People with Diabetes "At Risk" for Foot Ulceration

- Obtain protective shoes from an appropriately trained professional to ensure that they fit, protect, and accommodate your feet. Go to a pedorthist or a podiatrist and stay away from traveling salespeople, the internet, and mall kiosks for protective footwear.

- Enlist family members and caregivers to help you to remember to wear the shoes at all times, indoors and out.

- Check your feet every time you put on and take off your shoes.

- Check your shoes every time you take them off for puncture or foreign materials.

- If you have a foot deformity or a pre-ulcerative lesion on the bottom of your foot, consider the use of custom molded insoles that can offload high pressure areas and offer improved shock absorption and arch support.

- Have your podiatrist inspect your shoes every 3 months.

- Change out the soft insoles of your shoes every 3 to 4 months.

Other Factors to Consider

Getting properly fitted with therapeutic shoes unfortunately does not guarantee protection from ulceration. People at risk for foot ulceration need to develop an appreciation of how difficult it can be to heal a foot ulcer, with the possible results of infection, hospitalization, and in extreme cases, even amputation. Such an appreciation helps motivate people to take the necessary precautions to prevent wounds from occurring in the first place.

Sometimes people object to wearing protective shoes because they are not aesthetically pleasing or because the shoes are too difficult to put on. Whatever the reason, these objections should be addressed.

Many people, particularly the elderly, spend much of their time indoors. The potential for foot skin breakdown is as great inside the home, where hazards are always present, as outside of it. For instance, neuropathy might make a diabetic patient's bare foot insensitive to a foot injury, resulting in an unrecognized and unattended trauma. Therefore, it is critically important that shoes be worn in the house by "at-risk" people. Sometimes this is best accomplished with a different style shoe—one that can be more easily put on and taken off.

The Medicare Therapeutic Shoe Program

Medicare (and Medicare Advantage plans and some private insurance plans) provides coverage for protective shoes for people with diabetes who are considered to be "at risk" for foot ulceration. Risk factors include: (a) decreased sensation in the feet, (b) decreased blood flow to the feet, (c) a history of ulceration or deformity of the feet, and/or (d) amputation of the foot or part of the foot.

Medicare may provide a pair of protective shoes and up to three pairs of inserts every calendar year. Most people can be fitted with ready-made inserts that are heat molded to the shape of the arch. People with a more severe risk for ulceration are often fitted with custom inserts in order to provide extra protection.

If an "at-risk" foot is so irregularly shaped that it cannot be fitted into extra depth shoes, custom molded shoes are an option.

Talk with your podiatrist or your primary care doctor to see if you are "at risk" for foot ulcerations.

Socks

Socks provide an important interface between the foot and the shoe. As such, they offer (a) shock absorption, (b) friction and shear reduction, (c) moisture absorption, and (d) improved hygiene. Synthetic materials have replaced cotton and wool by offering superior wicking ability, breathability, and durability. It's important that socks not be too tight. White socks offer the benefit of more easily showing discoloration from drainage in the event of skin breakdown. Thicker socks offer superior cushioning and shock absorption, but they should be selected when the shoes are being sized to assure a proper fit.

Summary

Diabetes is associated with significantly increased risk for foot ulceration, infection, and amputation. The good news is that foot problems can be effectively prevented by the habits of daily foot inspections, regular visits to a podiatrist, and wearing appropriate shoes, socks, and inserts. People with diabetes should be evaluated annually to determine their level of ulcerative risk. People should know if they are found to be "at risk" and should have protective shoes that fit properly. People at risk should commit to wearing the special shoes whenever they are on their feet. Such an approach offers people with diabetes the best chance of living a long and active life, without unnecessary foot problems.

CHAPTER 8

Medications for the Diabetic Foot

This chapter provides a brief overview of medications available to treat the various conditions and complications associated with the diabetic foot. These medications should only be taken under the recommendation and supervision of your physician.

Diabetes is associated with the development of peripheral arterial disease (PAD). PAD results in decreased blood flow to the feet with a corresponding increase in issues with healing and the overall health of the foot. Medications used to treat PAD of the diabetic foot include:

1. Vasodilators: These medications act to increase the width of the blood vessels with a resulting increase in blood flow to the feet. One of the most common drugs in this class is Cilostazol (brand name: Pletal).

2. Blood Thinners: these medications decrease the clotting ability of the blood for increased flow to the feet. Common examples include aspirin and Clopidogrel (brand name: Plavix).

3. Blood Pressure Medications: High blood pressure is associated with increased complications with the diabetic foot. A blood pressure below 130/80 Hg is the goal of such medications.

4. Statins: High cholesterol and elevated triglycerides are associated with increased narrowing of the arteries of the diabetic foot. Statin medications decrease the production of these fatty substances by the liver.

Diabetes is associated with the development of peripheral neuropathy with numbness, pain, and loss of protective sensation to the feet. If the symptoms in your feet and legs begin to interfere with your quality of life or sleep, medication is often prescribed.

The best treatment for diabetic neuropathy involves getting and keeping your blood sugar under good control. If your Hemoglobin A1C test results decreases to below 7.0, the symptoms of diabetic neuropathy often subside. To minimize problems with diabetic neuropathy it's important to undertake additional measures, including exercising regularly, eating a healthy diet, getting quality sleep, and practicing stress management techniques.

(It is important to note that regulating your blood sugar is the best thing you can do for your diabetic feet. The medications used to accomplish this are beyond the scope of this book; your doctor and health care team can advise you.)

The pain and discomfort associated with diabetic neuropathy can sometimes become so severe that medication is required.

Two oral medications have been approved by the FDA for the treatment of painful peripheral neuropathy:

- Pregabalin (brand name: Lyrica) is an anti-convulsant given at 300 to 600 mg per day to help alleviate discomfort.
- Duloxetine (brand name: Cymbalta) is an antidepressant that can relieve the symptoms of nerve-related foot pain.

Other medications such as Gabapentin and Amitriptyline are often used for neuropathic foot pain. It is important to note that all of these medications have significant side effects, including weight gain and decreased mental acuity, and also typically have limited effectiveness. Therefore, there is a heightened threshold for the use of these medicines, and your doctor should prescribe the lowest possible dose to achieve the intended effects.

Topical medications such as Lidocaine and Capsaicin can be used for short-term pain relief. In a controlled study, compounded creams that contain multiple medications such as Gabapentin, Baclofen, ketamine, phenytoin, etc., have never been shown to provide superior results.

It should be noted that narcotic medications such as hydrocodone are no longer a third-line treatment in the protocol for painful diabetic neuropathy, due to their potential for abuse and addiction.

It is important for all your doctors to know which medications you are taking and equally important that *one* of your doctors is your "Medication Manager" who reviews and adjusts your medications to prevent duplication, to minimize side effects, and to avoid contraindications. Your pharmacist can also help you in this regard.

CHAPTER 9

Alternative Therapies for the Diabetic Foot

Peaople often want to treat themselves for medical issues, often to save money, or perhaps because a trusted friend or relative has raved about the benefits of a so-called cure-all. While this is understandable, there are risks involved with using unproven therapies, including side effects, interactions with other drugs, and wasting money on remedies that just plain don't work. Therefore, people with diabetes should always get the advice and consent of their doctor prior to beginning the use of "alternative" therapies, non-prescription vitamins and herbs, and other "home remedies."

The following is a list of supplements that have been tried by diabetics to improve their condition:

1. Alpha Lipoic Acid – This can be given orally or through a vein and may improve nerve function and decrease blood

sugar. Studies have not defined when this substance is needed or helpful.

2. Benfotiamine – This is a derivative of Thiamine (B1) and can truly help *some* people with diabetic neuropathy (but not others).

3. CBD Oil – Cannabidiol (CBD) Oil is a non-intoxicating derivative of the cannabis plant. Proponents of the use of this plant extract claim that the oil can relieve pain when rubbed on the skin and help with anxiety and stress when ingested orally. Currently, there is only anecdotal evidence to back these claims. In addition to the lack of regulations regarding the manufacturing standards of CBD products, there are also legal issues in many states.

4. Cinnamon – This spice may lower blood pressure and decrease blood sugar and inflammation, or it may not— studies are inconclusive. High doses may be toxic and cinnamon may alter the effectiveness of medications such as blood thinners and heart and digestive medications.

5. Chromium – This mineral may aid in decreasing blood glucose levels and improving insulin sensitivity. Talk to your doctor about chromium if you feel that you may not be eating enough of it and want to try a supplement.

6. Fiber – Fiber supplements can help you feel fuller without adding many calories. Your doctor can help you choose a fiber product that is right for you.

7. Fish Oil – Omega-3 fish oil supplements may be helpful in improving heart health and lowering blood pressure and inflammation.

8. Magnesium – This mineral is helpful as a stomach antacid and as a laxative, and for people with a magnesium deficiency. It may be helpful for treating high cholesterol, fibromyalgia, and restless leg syndrome.

9. Melatonin – This is a hormone taken primarily to help people sleep. It may also help alleviate chronic fatigue syndrome, anxiety, and restless leg syndrome. While safe, it has an effect on blood sugar and interacts negatively with several blood pressure medications. Melatonin should not be taken in addition to prescribed sleep medications such as zolpidem (brand name: Ambien) and lorazepam (brand name: Ativan).

10. Metanx – This is a prescription medical food used for diabetic peripheral neuropathy that includes vitamins B1, B9, B12, and folate. High doses of these nutrients are thought to increase the circulation and oxygen to the nerves, resulting in a decrease of symptoms. Many people seem to note an increased feeling of well-being while taking this supplement.

11. Polyphenols – These nutrients are found in certain foods, such as dark chocolate, blueberries, and green tea. Polyphenols have unknown health benefits but seem to be associated with weight loss, smooth digestion, and well-functioning nerve and vascular systems. It is generally better to eat polyphenol food than it is to take polyphenol supplements.

12. Vitamin B Complex – The "B" vitamins include B6, B 12, folic acid, niacin, pantothenic acid, riboflavin, and thiamine.

These vitamin supplements help not only people with deficiencies but also people with alcoholism, poor diets, and illnesses such as neuropathy. This type of product might help you if you have bothersome neuropathy.

13. Vitamin D – The sun, of course, is the best source of vitamin D. People that are older and/or do not get out into the direct sunlight are more prone to vitamin D deficiency. Vitamin D promotes bone health and healing and is associated with decreased falls and possibly decreased pain. People with hardened arteries and declining kidney function should use this supplement with caution.

Again, consultation with your doctor or pharmacist is necessary prior to starting any new vitamin or "nerve improvement" supplement for people with diabetes.

Home Remedies

Soaking the feet (but not burning them with water that is too hot) and applying heating creams (such as Capsaicin) or cooling gels (such as Biofreeze) may give temporary relief from neuropathy pain. Compression socks can decrease the nerve-related aggravation for many people. Gently rubbing your feet and legs with a back-washing brush can provide dilation of the skin and relief from painful neuropathy symptoms.[1]

Massage Therapy

Massage is useful for diabetic neuropathy pain by loosening and stretching the soft tissues of the feet and legs. Massage therapy can relieve the burning, numbness, or tingling of neuropathy for some people. The act of massaging the tissues also increases circulation to the legs and feet, which can help the health of the nerves over time.

Acupuncture

Acupuncture involves inserting small needles into the body at precise points to encourage the body to improve function and promote natural healing.

The benefits of acupuncture, which originated in ancient China, stem from the pseudoscientific explanation that needling these precise points stimulates the nervous system to release chemicals and hormones that can decrease pain or improve bodily functions. Acupressure is a variant technique whereby pressure is applied to these points instead of needles. While there is no definite proof that this type of treatment helps diabetic neuropathy, it is generally considered safe if performed by a properly credentialed practitioner.

Neuroelectrical Stimulation

There are various machines available on the Internet or by prescription that can "stimulate" the nerves of the lower extremities. The best of these devices improve nerve health by delivering more oxygen and nutrients to the nerves by increasing circulation and decreasing edema. Note that "TENS Units" do not meet this standard. The "PDC Restorer" and the "Neurogenx" devices are good examples of these therapies, which help many but not all people with painful neuropathy. Diabetics that do not want to take medication for painful foot neuropathy are good candidates for this type of therapy. Neuroelectrical therapy is typically not covered by medical insurance and often requires several weeks of regular treatments.

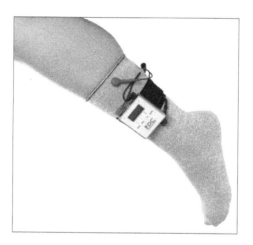

Light Therapy

Some neuropathy clinics offer low-level infrared light therapy designed to stimulate circulation and thus lessen the neuropathy symptoms in the feet and legs of their patients. Low level cold laser machines and the Anodyne infrared energy device are two examples of this technology. Many people report relief from neuropathy pain using this type of therapy. You can also buy smaller versions of these devices on the Internet. Since these treatments are often not covered by insurance, ask for a limited free trial if you decide to try this safe but unproven therapy.

Exercise Therapy

Exercise is listed again here because many of the alternative therapies listed above seek to relieve your symptoms by increasing the blood flow to the feet and legs, and that's what exercise can do. Exercise, with the proper shoes and the proper precautions, is free and has many positive side effects. It will lower your blood sugar and help with weight control. If you can break a sweat, you will release endorphins and that is always a good thing! We recommend that everyone walk at least twenty minutes per day—rain, snow, or shine.

Reference for Further Reading

1 Skaug, James D, *Peripheral Neuropathy; Case Histories, Myths, and Treatments that Work!*, Holistic Health Care Press, 2017.

CHAPTER 10

Diabetic Foot Wound Care

D iabetic foot ulcers (DFU) are defined as skin breakdown with exposure of the underlying tissue. These wounds eventually occur in approximately 25% of all diabetic patients (1). This complication of diabetes is recognized to be one of the most common yet potentially catastrophic consequences of the disease. DFUs also represent one of the most expensive healthcare burdens to treat in our society; costs are skyrocketing in excess of $15 billion annually (2). Diabetic foot ulcerations pose a significant threat to the affected patient in the absence of appropriate care. These complications include infection, hospitalization, amputation, and death. The majority of all lower extremity amputations are due to complications of diabetes and the direct result of an unhealed diabetic foot ulcer (3-5).

Thus, it is critically important to acknowledge the need for aggressive evaluation and management of ANY wound affecting the foot of a diabetic patient. Diabetic wound care is an effort to prevent disastrous complications. The management of diabetic foot ulcers is not nearly aggressive enough in many cases by both the patient and the provider.

Diabetic foot ulcers are a challenge to treat. The effects of diabetes on wound healing are extremely negative and quite complex, often resulting in poor healing and low closure rates. Often, a multidisciplinary approach (meaning the collaboration of several medical specialties working together) is required to provide successful wound care. It is the goal of this review to discuss general principles regarding wound formation, as well as to provide a brief overview of evidence-based protocols regarding treatment options, which you may wish to further discuss with your physician. Overall, improvement in patient education should lead to an improvement in patient care and subsequently result in the improvement of patient outcomes. In the case of diabetes and diabetic foot ulcerations, this means fewer infections, fewer hospitalizations, lower amputation rates, and improved success in preventing recurrence of a wound once a patient's DFU has been healed.

High Blood Sugar

Hyperglycemia, an excess of glucose (sugar) in the bloodstream, is a primary reason for the non-healing of diabetic foot wounds. The importance of glucose control is almost always underappreciated by the patient and understanding this concept is critical. Hemoglobin A1c (HA1c) tests provide an important measure of long-term glycemic control. Optimum HA1c levels for wound healing are generally recognized to be at or below 7%. While a HA1c percentage may display good overall glycemic control, even brief episodes of hyperglycemia (above 200mg/dL) can impair wound healing. Thus, blood sugar spikes should be avoided as much as possible by people with diabetic foot ulcers. Diligent glucose control *is a chief concern* with respect to the likelihood of achieving wound closure. This responsibility largely falls on the patient and requires them to be active in their treatment. Glucose control can be discussed with a patient's primary care provider or endocrinologist as it relates to the need for strict control during treatment of a diabetic foot ulcer. Alterations in a patient's current medication regimen may be necessary. Often, a patient's adherence to medication, diet, and other lifestyle guidelines are required to achieve glycemic control. This effort should be thought of as a partnership between the patient and their doctors, with each of the partners having responsibilities and duties in achieving the end goal of wound healing.

The quintessential reference for diabetic wound care was updated in February 2016 in the *Journal of Vascular Surgery* (6), which outlined current practice recommendations and protocols for clinicians in treating DFU. This article is referenced for the reader to demonstrate that the following recommendations are the "best-practice guidelines" reported by evidence-based medicine standards.

Blood Flow

A pillar of appropriate diabetic wound care is the assessment and management of the vascular status of the patient. This means assessing how much blood flow is getting down to a patient's foot and to the wound itself. Hyperglycemia can decrease the amount of circulation to the feet, leading to a medical condition called peripheral arterial disease (PAD). Poor blood circulation is a major concern for patients with non-healing diabetic foot ulcerations. Often, this is a major hurdle in wound healing in the diabetic foot.

The signs and symptoms of PAD of the feet and lower legs must be assessed. The diminished or complete absence of palpable pedal pulses strongly suggests the presence of PAD. Noninvasive vascular tests called ankle-brachial indices (ABI) or toe-brachial indices (TBI) can help detect peripheral vascular disease. Referral to a vascular specialist for additional evaluation and consideration of surgical bypass or endovascular interventions are required when blood flow is determined to be an issue in healing diabetic foot ulcers.

Debridement

Sharp surgical debridement remains a "best practice" for diabetic foot ulcer management and wound healing. Surgical debridement involves removing the devitalized and dead tissues within the wound as well as the bacteria causing infection around and directly inside the wound. This procedure increases the rate of new tissue development, decreases any infection present, and speeds wound healing. A very influential study demonstrated that frequency of debridement was directly proportional to the rate of healing—the more frequent the debridement, the faster the rate of healing (7). Surgical debridement performed at weekly intervals produces the largest closure and healing rates for chronic wounds. An alternative to surgical debridement using a topical medication

(Santyl) that enzymatically debrides the wound is sometimes needed for home use.

Offloading

Perhaps the most often overlooked necessity to healing diabetic wounds on the bottom of the feet is adequate offloading of pressure from the wound. Simply stated, if there was sufficient pressure to create the wound, new tissue and skin have virtually no chance at reforming unless the pressure on the wound is dramatically reduced. Redistribution of pressure away from the area of ulceration is critical. The gold standard in wound offloading is the total contact cast (TCC). Unfortunately, high cost, technical difficulty with applications, and inconvenience has led to this treatment modality being underutilized. Patient willingness to undergo weekly casting can be an issue also, as many patients do not want to be burdened with having to wear a cast that makes daily routines and walking more difficult. Simply stated, TCCs should be utilized more frequently. Alternatives to TCC include walking boots, offloading sandals and shoe inserts, and instructions to stay non-weight bearing with the assistance of crutches, walkers, or wheelchair devices. While these methods can be effective, studies show that patients do not keep the weight off of the healing wound the majority of the time using them (8). Unfortunately, patient adherence to non-weight bearing on wounds is often implicated in the failure to heal the wound.

Topical Medications and Adjuncts

The number of products available for healing diabetic wounds is overwhelming. There is insufficient evidence to recommend any specific product for DFUs. The basic principle is to keep the wound clean and moist. Availability, ease of use, and cost of products are part of the selection process. There is no wound care dressing or topical medication that will singularly succeed without the previously described pillars of wound care: 1) adequate blood flow to the foot, 2) frequent debridement of the wound bed, and 3) substantial and *consistent* offloading of the wound.

Diabetic foot ulcerations which fail to decrease in size by at least 50% over a period of four weeks should be reassessed and the treatment regimen should be altered (9). Continuation of the current therapy without change will likely fail in this circumstance. Wound measurements and assessment should be performed each week before and after debridement, with complete reevaluation performed every four weeks to look at the reduction in the size of the wound over the previous four weeks. If appropriate wound closure rates are not achieved, adjunctive or advanced wound care therapies may be indicated. These may include negative pressure wound therapy (NPWT), advanced biologic dressings, and hyperbaric oxygen supplementation, among many others.

It is often said that "the best offense is a good defense." This is an accurate statement regarding the importance of preventing the development of diabetic foot ulcerations, or preventing a diabetic foot ulcer from forming again once it has healed. One tidbit for ulcer prevention is offered here from Jonathan Brantley, DPM (10): "The protective insoles of the footwear of at-risk patients should be covered in pink plastazote, as this material closely mimics the tensile strength and durability of human skin. One should inspect the pink plastazote lining of the diabetic insole for any tethering, compression, or tears—if damage to the insole lining is present, it means your skin is next! Prevention of diabetic foot ulcers should be of paramount importance and pink plastazote represents a very effective forecasting tool."

Summary

Optimization of glucose control, adequate blood flow levels in the lower extremity, frequent (weekly) wound debridement, and constant pressure relief to the area of ulceration should all be addressed as part of an effective wound care protocol. Diabetic foot ulcerations that fail to demonstrate a 50% reduction in size after four weeks should be reassessed and the current treatment plan modified to possibly include more aggressive therapies. Diabetic foot ulcer treatment is challenging as diabetes negatively affects wound healing in numerous ways. Repercussions of diabetic foot ulcerations can be severe, mandating the need for optimum wound care treatments and effective subsequent interventions aimed at the prevention of wound recurrence.

References for Further Reading

1. Frykberg RG, Zgonis T, Armstrong DG, et al. Diabetic foot disorders. A clinical practice guideline (2006 revision). *J Foot Ankle Surg* 2006;45:S1–S66. Crossref, Medline, Google Scholar

2. Al-Maskari F., El-Sadig M. Prevalence of risk factors for diabetic foot complications. *BMC Family Practice.* 2007; 8:p. 59

3. Robbins, Jeffrey & Strauss, Gerald & Aron, David & Long, Jodi & Kuba, Jennifer & Kaplan, Yelena. (2008). Mortality Rates and

Diabetic Foot Ulcers Is it Time to Communicate Mortality Risk to Patients with Diabetic Foot Ulceration? Journal of the American Podiatric Medical Association. 98. 489-93. 10.7547/0980489.

4. Boulton AJ, Vileikyte L, Ragnarson-Tennvall G, et al. The global burden of diabetic foot disease. *Lancet* 2005; 366: 1719-1724.

5. Frykberg RG. Diabetic foot ulcers: pathogenesis and management. *Am Fam Physician* 2002; 66(9): 1655-62.

6. Hingorani A, LaMuraglia GM, Henke P, et al. The management of diabetic foot: a clinical practice guideline by the Society for Vascular Surgery in collaboration with the American Podiatric Medical Association and the Society of Vascular Medicine. *J Vasc Surg.* 2016; 63(2 Suppl):3S-21S.

7. Wilcox JR, Carter MJ, Covington S. Frequency of Debridements and Time to Heal: A Retrospective Cohort Study of 312,744 Wounds. *JAMA Dermatol.* 2013; 149(9):1050–1058. doi:10.1001/jamadermatol.2013.4960.

8. Armstrong DG, Lavery LA, Kimbriel HR, et al. Activity patterns of patients with diabetic foot ulceration: patients with active ulceration may not adhere to a standard pressure offloading regimen. *Diabetes Care* 2003; 26: 12595-97.

9. Sheehan, Peter, Jones, Peter, Caselli, Antonella, et al. Percent Change in Wound Area of Diabetic Foot Ulcers Over a 4-Week Period Is a Robust Predictor of Complete Healing in a 12-Week Prospective Trial. *Diabetes Care* Jun 2003, 26 (6) 1879-1882; DOI: 10.2337/diacare.26.6.1879.

10. Brantley, Jonathan N., Richmond Virginia, personal communication.

CHAPTER 11

Diabetic Foot Surgery

Diabetic foot surgery has more complications than other foot surgeries, statistically speaking. Important considerations include the physical condition and testing results of the patient having surgery. Improved diabetic foot surgical success is likely to occur under the following conditions:

1. HgA1C of less than 8
2. Blood glucose at the time of surgery of less than 200 mg/dL
3. No fever
4. Sufficient blood flow and overall condition to tolerate the surgery and its recovery
5. Detailed instructions, gait training, foot exercises, and shoe modifications before the surgery
6. Close monitoring after the surgery for appropriate progress and healing

Elective diabetic foot surgery is sometimes indicated. Crooked toes, bunions, or prominent metatarsal bones may keep causing ulcers or infections. In such cases, a palliative procedure may be indicated to prevent future ulcerations. Diabetic feet in good condition, in conjunction with the application of the six recommendations listed above, can do very nicely with foot surgery.

People with severe peripheral neuropathy can actually break the bones and dislocate the joints of their feet and ankles. This condition was first described by French neurologist Jean-Martin Charcot in the 1800s and is commonly known as "Charcot Foot." Charcot Foot leads to a grossly deformed foot that is especially prone to breakdown. Thus, people with Charcot Foot are required to wear large braces and severely limit weight-bearing on the foot for the rest of their lives. Reconstructive surgery that restores better alignment to the foot is a consideration for Charcot Foot patients in relatively good shape. Consultation with doctors having extensive experience with this surgery is recommended in these circumstances.

Peripheral arterial disease (PAD) develops in the diabetic foot more often than the non-diabetic foot. PAD can lead to an important artery supplying blood to the foot becoming clogged—putting the foot at risk for gangrene and amputation. To open up the clogged artery, a vascular surgeon can perform procedures such as:

1. Angioplasty – A small incision is used to insert a balloon that is inflated at the site of artery blockage to open the artery up and/or to insert a stent to hold the artery open to restore blood flow to the foot.

2. Bypass – A new passage for blood flow to the foot is created around a relatively large section of blockage of an artery using another blood vessel or a synthetic graft to improve blood flow to the foot.

3. Clot Busting – A medication can be injected at the location of the closed artery to break up the clot that has formed to improve blood flow to the foot.

One area of diabetic foot surgery that needs further study is nerve decompression surgery, whereby the major nerves of the foot and leg are delicately "released" from surrounding structures. The purpose of this surgery is to decrease the symptoms and improve the sensation of people with diabetic sensory neuropathy. Many doctors are skeptical of the efficacy of this surgery because diabetic neuropathy is thought to be caused by too much sugar in the blood, which leads to malfunction of the nerves. However, it is true that people with diabetes tend to have more compression neuropathies than people without diabetes. Thus, there may be a subset of diabetics who could benefit from this type of procedure. More studies are needed to determine who could benefit from these "nerve decompression" operations.

CHAPTER 12

Diabetic Foot Pathway for Monitoring and Care

P eople with diabetes should have an initial detailed Diabetic Foot Examination performed by a podiatrist. Based on the findings of this examination, the need for additional monitoring, testing, and treatment of the feet will be determined.

Every person with diabetes should know which of the five classes below they fall into based on the findings of their annual foot examination. These patients should follow the checklist associated with their class. If a person's feet fall into more than one class (for example, the feet have both impaired circulation and impaired sensation), both class checklists should be used.

1. **Foot examination with no significant findings.** If the detailed foot examination reveals no problems with the blood flow, the nerve function, or the structure of the foot, the following checklist should be used:

    a. Review the Foot Exam Findings

    b. Review Diabetic Foot Care Fundamentals

    c. Review and apply the Diabetic Foot Wellness Program*

    d. Schedule a Detailed Foot Examination in one year. This is especially important if the person has risk factors for diabetic foot complications including any of the following:

        a) a HgA1C of greater than 7.0,

        b) a BMI of over 25,

        c) a smoking habit,

        d) hypertension, or

        e) an age of over 50 years.

2. **Foot Examination reveals the signs and symptoms of arterial disease.** If the Foot Examination reveals decreased blood flow to the feet, via symptoms such as calf pain with walking, or warning signs such as diminished foot pulses, cool toes, etc., the following checklist should be used:

    a. Review the Foot Exam findings with the patient

    b. Review or obtain the results of Ankle Brachial Indices and/or Microcirculation testing and consider the referral of the patient to a vascular specialist

    c. Review Diabetic Foot Care Fundamentals

    d. Review and Apply the Diabetic Foot Wellness Program

    e. Start a prescribed Diabetic Foot Exercise program

    f. Schedule periodic prophylactic foot care visits as needed (usually every 2 to 3 months)

    g. Check and possibly modify or replace the patient's footwear for preventive purposes

h. Schedule an annual follow-up Detailed Foot Examination

3. **Foot Examination reveals problems with the nerves of the feet.** If the Foot Examination reveals diminished sensation to the feet, especially with the loss of protective sensation, the following checklist should be used:

   a. Review the Findings of the Foot Exam with the patient
   b. Review Diabetic Foot Care Fundamentals
   c. Review and Apply the Diabetic Foot Wellness Program
   d. Start a prescribed Diabetic Foot Exercise Program
   e. Review or initiate a Protective Footwear Program
   f. Schedule periodic prophylactic foot care visits as needed (typically every 2 to 6 months)
   g. Schedule an annual follow-up Diabetic Foot Examination

4. **Foot Examination reveals structural problems with the feet.** If the foot examination reveals foot deformities such as hammertoes or bunions, the following checklist should be applied:

   a. Review the findings of the Foot Exam with the patient
   b. Review Diabetic Foot Care Fundamentals
   c. Review and Apply the Diabetic Foot Wellness Program
   d. Review or initiate a Protective Footwear Program
   e. If the pedal circulation is adequate, consider surgical correction of the deformity to prevent future problems
   f. Schedule an annual follow-up Diabetic Foot Examination

5. **Foot Examination reveals prior non-traumatic amputation or chronic foot wound.** If the patient has had a partial or complete foot amputation due to impaired circulation or

a foot infection, more vigilant foot monitoring is required to prevent additional problems. People who have had a chronic wound on their foot in the past also require additional monitoring and care to prevent a new wound from developing. The following checklist should be applied in these two circumstances:

a. Review the findings of the Foot Exam with the patient
b. Review Diabetic Foot Care Fundamentals
c. Review and apply the Diabetic Foot Wellness Program
d. Start a prescribed Diabetic Foot Exercise Program
e. Review or initiate a Protective Footwear Program
f. Schedule periodic prophylactic foot care visits (usually every 1 to 3 months)
g. Schedule a semiannual Diabetic Foot Examination

The Diabetic Foot Wellness Program includes information and instructions given to patients via educational handouts and video on how to optimize the health of their feet. Topics covered under this program include:

- Exercise
- Nutrition
- Weight Loss
- Smoking Cessation
- Stress Management
- Quality Sleep

One-page handouts summarizing these topics can be found in the Appendices. Consultation with a Certified Diabetes Educator is also encouraged as part of this program.

APPENDICES

You can download printable 8.5 x 11 inch versions of these appendices at www.instridefoot.com.

Just for fun, how about you do a 3-week Foot Exercise program and a 3-week Diet Log program and see what kinds of positive changes take place for you?

Diabetic Foot Care Fundamentals

FOOT CARE FUNDAMENTALS

Good blood sugar control – Know your HgA1c number (and your target HgA1c number).

Inspect your feet daily — look for cuts, blisters, redness, swelling, or nail problem.

Keep your feet clean and healthy — wash them daily with soap and dry them carefully, especially between the toes. Use moisturizer on your lower legs and feet regularly (except between the toes).

Be very careful when soaking your feet — especially if you have neuropathy.

Visit a podiatrist — at least annually for a foot inspection.

Find out if your feet are "at risk". — If your feet are "at risk", turn your foot care over to your podiatrist. If your feet are not "at risk", carefully trim and file smooth your toenails.

Always wear the proper shoes and socks. — If your feet are "at risk", wear your protective footwear — never go barefoot. Check the insides of your shoes before you put them on.

Avoid tobacco use — if you smoke, quit.

Exercise on a regular basis — go for a walk every day.

Know your Diabetic Foot Category — 1) No Significant Issue, 2) Impaired Nerve Function, 3) Impaired Blood Flow to the feet (PAD), 4) Structural Deformity of the feet, and 5) Prior foot ulcer and/or amputation — this category requires extra special attention.

APPENDIX 2

Prescription for Diabetic Foot Exercises

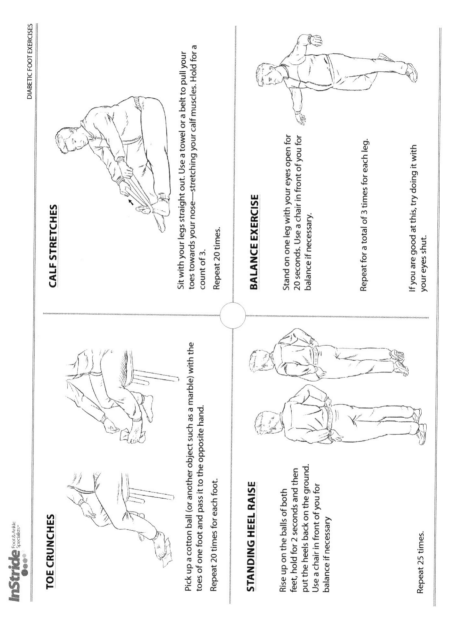

CALF STRETCHES

Sit with your legs straight out. Use a towel or a belt to pull your toes towards your nose—stretching your calf muscles. Hold for a count of 3.

Repeat 20 times.

BALANCE EXERCISE

Stand on one leg with your eyes open for 20 seconds. Use a chair in front of you for balance if necessary.

Repeat for a total of 3 times for each leg.

If you are good at this, try doing it with your eyes shut.

TOE CRUNCHES

Pick up a cotton ball (or another object such as a marble) with the toes of one foot and pass it to the opposite hand.

Repeat 20 times for each foot.

STANDING HEEL RAISE

Rise up on the balls of both feet, hold for 2 seconds and then put the heels back on the ground. Use a chair in front of you for balance if necessary

Repeat 25 times.

InStride Foot & Ankle Specialists

84

APPENDIX 3

Monthly Log for Foot Exercises

MONTHLY FOOT EXERCISE LOG   MONTH: _____

EXERCISE	DAYS OF THE MONTH																														
	1	2	3	4	5	6	7	8	9	10	11	12	13	14	15	16	17	18	19	20	21	22	23	24	25	26	27	28	29	30	31
20-Minute Walk																															
Toe Crunches																															
Standing Heel Raise																															
Calf Stretches																															
Balance Exercise																															

InStride Foot & Ankle Specialists

85

APPENDIX 4

The Plate Method

HEALTHY EATING VIA THE "PLATE METHOD"

There is no one set diet for people with diabetes. The "Plate Method" depicted below gives a straightforward, fundamental approach that will work for most people.

Basic Plate Approach Method to Meal Planning

Drink choice-low calorie, unsweetened

Fruit choice or dairy choice

Fill ¼ of your plate with a protein choice

Fill half of your meal plate with non-starchy, green leafy vegetables

Fill ¼ of your plate with starchy vegetables or whole grains

APPENDIX 5
Weekly Diet Log

WEEKLY DIET LOG
(completed)

It is sometimes best to focus on 2 to 5 small changes in your diet rather than get too complicated. The Weekly Log below focuses four factors chosen as keys for the coming week. The next page will give you a clean copy to pick your own areas of focus. Ideas to consider are a) Lean meat choice b) No sugar or cream in coffee, c) Nothing Out of a Box, d) No Food after 7 pm, e) No candy and f) No fried food.

B is for Breakfast; L is for Lunch; D is for Dinner.

Name: _____ Date: _____ Score: _____

	Take Time Eating			No Sugar in Drinks			Veggies First on Plate			Fresh Food		
	B	L	D	B	L	D	B	L	D	B	L	D
Monday	✔											
Tuesday									✔			
Wednesday					✔							
Thursday												
Friday												
Saturday											✔	
Sunday												

APPENDIX 6

Foods to Choose and Foods to Avoid

SUGGESTED WELLNESS PROGRAM

RECOMMENDED FOODS	NOT RECOMMENDED FOOD
PROTEIN	
Plant-based proteins, such as beans, nuts, seeds, or tofu	Fried meats. Higher-fat cuts of meat. such as ribs
Fish and seafood	Pork bacon, Deep-fried tofu
Chicken and other poultry (Choose the breast meat)	Regular cheeses, Beans prepared with lard
Eggs and low-fat	Poultry with skin, deep-fried fish
DAIRY	
1% or skim milk	Whole milk, regular ice cream, regular half-and-half
Low-fat yogurt, Low-fat cottage cheese	Regular yogurt, regular cottage cheese
Low-fat or nonfat sour cream	Regular sour cream
FATS, OILS, AND SWEETS	
Natural sources of vegetables fats, such as nuts, seeds, or avocados (high in calories, so keep portions small). Plant-based oils. such as canola,	Anything with artificial trans fat in it. Anything that's "partially hydrogenated", even if the label says it has 0 grams of trans fat.
Salmon, tuna, or mackerel. Natural sources of vegetable fats, such as nuts, seeds, or avocados (high in calories so keep portions small).	Big portions of saturated fats, which mainly come from animal products but also are in coconuts oil and palm oil.
DRINKS	
Water, unflavoured or flavoured sparkling water	Regular sodas
Unsweetened tea (add a slice of lemon)	Regular beer, fruity mixed drinks, dessert wines
Light beer, small amounts of wine, or non-fruity mixed drinks	Sweetened tea. Energy drinks
Coffee, black or with added low-fat milk and sugar substitute	Coffee with sugar and cream. Flavoured coffees and chocolate drinks.

Foods to Choose and Foods to Avoid

(CONTINUED)

RECOMMENDED FOODS	NOT RECOMMENDED FOOD
STARCHES	
Whole grains, such as brown rice, oatmeal, quinoa, millet or amaranth	Processed grains, such as white rice or white flour
Baked sweet potato	Cereals with little whole grains and lots of sugar
Item made with whole grains and no added sugar	White bread, french fries
VEGETABLES	
Fresh veggies, eaten raw or lightly steamed, roasted, or grilled	Canned vegetables with lots of added sodium
Plain frozen vegetables, lightly steamed	Veggies cooked with lots of added butter, cheese, or sauce
Greens such as kale, spinach and arugula. Iceberg lettuce is not as great, because its low in nutrients	Pickles, if you need to limit sodium - otherwise, pickles are okay
Low sodium or unsalted canned vegetables	Sauerkraut, for the same reason as pickles - so, limit them if you have high blood pressure
FRUITS	
Fresh fruit	Canned fruit with heavy sugar syrup
Plain frozen fruit or fruit canned without added sugar	Chewy fruit rolls
Sugar-free or low-sugar jam or preserves	Regular jam, jelly, and preserves (unless you have a very small portion)
No-sugar-added applesauce	Sweetened applesauce, fruit punch, fruit drinks, fruit juice drinks

APPENDIX 7

Glycemic Food Index

GLYCEMIC INDEX CONTROL

WHAT IS THE GLYCEMIC INDEX (GI)?

The GI is one the best tools for fat loss. It measures how quickly foods breakdown into sugar in your bloodstream. High glycemic foods turn into blood sugar very quickly. Starchy foods like potatoes are a good example. Potatoes have such a high GI rating it's almost the same as eating table sugar.

WHAT IS THE GLYCEMIC LOAD (GL)?

It measures the amount of carbohydrate in each service of food. Foods with a GL under 10 are good choices. These foods should be your first choice for carts Foods that fall between 10 and 20 on the GL scale have a moderate effect on your blood sugar. Foods with a GL above 20 will cause blood sugar and insulin spikes.

TYPES OF FOOD	GLYCEMIC INDEX	SERVING SIZE	NET CARBS	GLYCEMIC LOAD
Peanuts	14	4 oz (113g)	15	2
Bean Sprouts	25	1 cup (104g)	4	1
Grapefruit	25	1/2 large (166g)	11	3
Apples	38	1 medium (138g)	16	6
Carrots	47	1 large (72g)	5	2
Oranges	48	1 medium (131g)	12	6
Pizza	30	2 slices (260g)	42	13
Lowfat Yogurt	33	1 cup (245g)	47	16
Spaghetti	42	1 cup (140g)	38	16
Bananas	52	1 large (136g)	27	14
Potato Chips	54	4 oz (114g)	55	30
Honey	55	1 tbsp (21g)	17	9
Sugar (sucrose)	68	1 tbsp (12g)	12	8
Oatmeal	58	1 cup (234g)	21	12
Ice Cream	61	1 cup (72g)	16	10
Snickers Bar	55	1 bar (113g)	64	35
Brown Rice	55	1 cup (195g)	42	23
Macaroni and Cheese	64	1 serving (166g)	47	30
Raisins	64	1 small box (43g)	32	20
White Rice	64	1 cup (186g)	52	33
Popcorn	72	2 cups (16g)	10	7
Watermelon	72	1 cup (154g)	11	8
White Bread	70	1 slice (30g)	14	10
Baked Potato	85	1 medium (173g)	43	28
Glucose	100	(50g)	50	50

Wellness, Quality Sleep, and Stress Relief

DIABETIC FOOT WELLNESS HABITS

1) A healthy lifestyle for people with diabetes includes the following:

   a) Good nutrition

   b) Maintain a healthy weight (know your BMI and your BMI goal)

   c) Daily exercise

   d) No smoking and limited alcohol use

   e) Stress management

   f) Preventive care

2) Quality sleep is very important. Tips for quality sleep include:

   a) Go to bed and awaken at consistent times (even on weekends)

   b) Keep your bedroom dark and cool

   c) No electronic devices before bed (TV, computer, phone)

   d) No naps during the daytime

   e) Regular exercise

   f) Avoid caffeine and alcohol before bed

3) Stress management practices should include:

   a) Exercise daily

   b) Meditate or do Deep Breathing Exercises daily

   c) Spend time outdoors every day

   d) Join a support group (or spend time with loved ones)

   e) Pursue a hobby that you enjoy

   f) Get enough quality sleep

   g) Celebrate all small successes that you have

APPENDIX 9

Smoking Cessation

FIVE KEYS FOR QUITTING	YOUR QUIT PLAN
1. GET READY.	**1. YOUR QUIT DATE:**
• Set a quit date and stick to it—not even a single puff!	
• Think about past quit attempts. What worked and what did not?	
2. GET SUPPORT AND ENCOURAGEMENT.	**2. WHO CAN HELP YOU:**
• Tell your family, friends, and coworkers you are quitting.	
• Talk to your doctor or other health care provider.	
• Get group, individual, or telephone counseling.	
3. LEARN NEW SKILLS AND BEHAVIORS.	**3. SKILLS AND BEHAVIORS YOU CAN USE:**
• When you first try to quit, change your routine.	
• Reduce stress.	
• Distract yourself from urges to smoke.	
• Plan something enjoyable to do every day.	
• Drink a lot of water and other fluids.	
4. GET MEDICATION AND USE IT CORRECTLY.	**4. YOUR MEDICATION PLAN:**
• Talk with your health care provider about which medication will work best for you:	Medications: _____
• Bupropion SR—available by prescription.	Instructions: _____
• Nicotine gum available over-the-counter.	
• Nicotine inhaler—available by prescription.	
• Nicotine nasal spray—available by prescription.	
• Nictone patch available over-the-counter.	
5. BE PREPARED FOR RELAPSE OR DIFFICULT SITUATIONS.	**5. HOW WILL YOU PREPARE?**
• Avoid alcohol.	
• Be careful around other smokers.	
• Improve your mood in ways other than smoking.	
• Eat a healthy diet and stay active.	

APPENDIX 10

Footwear Recommendations

FOOTWEAR REQUIREMENTS
FOR PEOPLE WITH DIABETES

Feature	Requirements
Length	Inner length of the footwear should be 1 to 2 cm longer than the foot length as measured from heel to the longest toe when a person is standing. Adequate length needs to be confirmed when people are weight-bearing while wearing the footwear.
Depth	Depth should accommodate the toes to move freely without causing pressure at the medial, lateral, or the dorsal surfaces of the foot.
Width	Width should equal the width of all parts of the foot. Width is good when the upper can be slightly bunched. The relation between forefoot and rearfoot is important, as accommodating a wide forefoot may result in the heel being too wide.
Height	Footwear height can be low, ankle-high, or high. High footwear provides more firmness, stability, and reduces joint motion. The shaft of high footwear also contributes to forefoot pressure reduction. See Table 3 for specific height requirements for people with a foot deformity.
Insole	The removable molded insole can be pre-fabricated or custom-made. The primary function of the insole is pressure redistribution. This is achieved via the principle of increasing the contact area between the foot and the insole, and the addition of corrective elements in the insole. Shock-absorbing, soft, but sufficiently resilient and non-slippery materials should be used.
Outsole	Rubber, plastic, and leather can all be used in construction of footwear outsoles, but rubber outsoles are thought to be superior. Outsoles can be supple, toughened, or stiff. The shoe should not be more supple than the foot, or friction between foot and shoe will develop during push-off. See Table 3 for specific outsole requirements for people with a foot deformity and Table 4 for the offloading effects of specific modifications.
Length	Inner length of the footwear should be 1 to 2 cm longer than the foot length as measured from heel to the longest toe when a person is standing. Adequate length needs to be confirmed when people are weight-bearing while wearing the footwear.
Depth	Depth should accommodate the toes to move freely without causing pressure at the medial, lateral, or the dorsal surfaces of the foot.

Footwear Recommendations

(CONTINUED)

Feature	Requirements
Width	Width should equal the width of all parts of the foot. Width is good when the upper can be slightly bunched. The relation between forefoot and rearfoot is important, as accommodating a wide forefoot may result in the heel being too wide.
Height	Footwear height can be low, ankle-high, or high. High footwear provides more firmness, stability, and reduces joint motion. The shaft of high footwear also contributes to forefoot pressure reduction. See Table 3 for specific height requirements for people with a foot deformity.
Insole	The removable molded insole can be pre-fabricated or custom-made. The primary function of the insole is pressure redistribution. This is achieved via the principle of increasing the contact area between the foot and the insole, and the addition of corrective elements in the insole. Shock-absorbing, soft, but sufficiently resilient and non-slippery materials should be used.
Outsole	Rubber, plastic, and leather can all be used in construction of footwear outsoles, but rubber outsoles are thought to be superior. Outsoles can be supple, toughened, or stiff. The shoe should not be more supple than the foot, or friction between foot and shoe will develop during push-off. See Table 3 for specific outsole requirements for people with a foot deformity and Table 4 for the offloading effects of specific modifications.
Rocker Profile	Rocker profiles have proven effective in reducing plantar pressures, especially on the forefoot. The rocker profile chosen depends on the affected joints and is determined by the apex position (pivot point) and the angle from the pivot point to the tip of the toe. For plantar pressure reduction of the metatarsophalangeal joints, the pivot point needs to be proximal to these joints. The rocker profile also impacts balance; the more proximally placed, the greater the balance disturbance. A person's balance should therefore always be taken into account when deciding on the rocker profile.
Heel Enclosure	An adequately fitting and enclosed heel is recommended, as open-backed footwear or a heel enclosure that is too wide can result in injury and usually requires a person to claw their toes in order to keep them on. The heel counter needs to be free of edges protruding into the footwear.
Heel Lift	The heel lift (or heel-forefoot difference, or pitch) should be generally 1.5–2 cm, and should not exceed 3 cm.

Footwear Recommendations

(CONTINUED)

Feature	Requirements
Closure	Adequate closure (or fixation) is needed to keep the foot from sliding forward. Closure should allow secure longer-term fastening and individual adjustment. Laces have long been considered the optimal choice; however, alternatives that are easier to use while still meeting these criteria are available as well, and innovative closures continue to be developed.
Uppers	The uppers consist of the "quarter" (hind- and midfoot) and "vamp" (forefoot and toes). Uppers should be made from leather or a combination of materials (similar to sports shoes), with smooth inner lining made from a material that does not harden over time, with limited seams and preferably no seams in the vamp area as they reduce the ability of the leather to give. Uppers should be breathable and durable and have the ability to mold to deformities of the foot without resulting in pressure areas. Uppers can be supple, toughened, or stiff. The vamp area should generally remain supple to accommodate the toes. See Table 3 for specific requirements for the uppers (quarter) for people with a foot deformity.
Toe Box	The part of the shoe that covers and protects the toes. This should be supple (unless specific requirements, e.g., for building professionals, require otherwise), and should accommodate the shape of the toes to avoid any rubbing on the toes.

The Anatomy of a Shoe

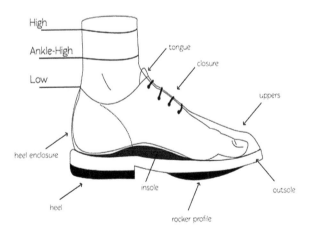

Footwear Recommendations

(CONTINUED)

Specific Footwear Requirements for People
with Diabetes and a Foot Deformity

	Height	Outsole	Uppers (quarter)[b]	Tongue
Limited joint mobility	Low[a]	Toughened	Supple	Supple
Pes cavus	Ankle-high	Toughened	Toughened	Toughened[c]
Flexible flat foot with hallux valgus	High	Toughened	Toughened	Toughened[c]
Rigid flat foot with hallux valgus	Ankle-high	Toughened	Strong medial support	Toughened[c]
Charcot foot	High	Stiff	Toughened	Toughened[c]
Hallux or toe amputation	High	Stiff	Toughened	Toughened[c]
Forefoot amputation	High	Stiff	Stiff	Stiff

Van Netten, et. al., Journal of Foot and Ankle Research, 2018, volume 11, Issue 2. http://creativecommons.org/licenses/by/4.0/

APPENDIX 11

Diabetic Foot Management Pathway

DIABETIC FOOT PATHWAY
FOR MANAGEMENT AND CARE

Every person with diabetes should have a detailed annual foot examination and know which of the following categories their feet belong to:

1. No Significant Problems
   - Review Foot Exam Findings and Foot Care Fundamentals
   - Work on Wellness
2. Signs and Symptoms of Peripheral Arterial Disease
   - Review Foot Exam Findings and Foot Care Fundamentals
   - Consider referring the patient to a vascular specialist
   - Work on Wellness
   - Daily Prescribed Exercise Program
   - Prophylactic Foot Care Program (4 to 6 visits per year)
   - Evaluate and Modify Footwear
3. Signs and Symptoms of Peripheral Neuropathy
   - Review Foot Exam Findings and Foot Care Fundamentals
   - Work on Wellness
   - Daily Exercise Program
   - Prophylactic Foot Care Program (2 to 6 visits per year)
   - Protective Footwear Program
4. Structural Problems with the Feet
   - Review Foot Exam Findings and Foot Care Fundamentals
   - Work on Wellness
   - Consider Surgical Correction of Deformities (with good circulation)
5. Prior Amputation or History of Foot Ulcer
   - Review Foot Exam Findings and Foot Care Fundamentals
   - Work on Wellness
   - Daily Prescribed Exercise Program
   - Prophylactic Foot Care Program (6 to 12 visits per year)
   - Protective Footwear Program

The Wellness Program mentioned above includes the following:
   - Blood Sugar Control (with a target HgA1c)
   - Exercise
   - Diet and Weight Management
   - Quality Sleep
   - Stress Management
   - Smoking Cessation

References and Resources

Videos

You can find Companion Videos to this book at the "InStride Foot" YouTube channel on the following topics:

    i.   Diabetic Foot Care Fundamentals

    ii. Diabetic Foot Assessment

    iii. Diabetic Foot Exercises

    iv. Diabetic Nutrition and Wellness

    v.   Wellness, Quality Sleep, and Stress Relief

    vi. Footwear Recommendations

    vii. Diabetic Peripheral Neuropathy

References

American Diabetes Association, *Diagnosis and Management of Diabetic Foot Complications*, ADA, 2018.

American Diabetes Association, *Microvascular Complications and Foot Care, Diabetes Care*, 2017.

American Diabetes Association, Standards of Medical Care in Diabetes – 2018, *Clinical Diabetes*, 2018.

American Diabetes Association, *Your Health Care Team*, www.diabetes.org, 2018.

American Diabetes Association, *Dietary Supplements: Side Effects and Drug Interactions*, www.diabetes.org, 2014.

Armstrong, DG and Lavery, LA, *Clinical Care of the Diabetic Foot*, American Diabetes Association, 2016.

Columbo, Joseph, et al, *Clinical Autonomic Dysfunction*, Springer Publishing, 2015.

Diabetic Foot Australia guidelines on Footwear for People with Diabetes, Jaap J. van Netten, et.al., Journal of foot and Ankle Research, 2018, Volume 11, Issue 2.

Wiesman, Janice F., *Peripheral Neuropathy*, John Hopkins Press, 2016.

National Diabetes Information Clearinghouse, *Diabetic Neuropathies: The Nerve Damage of Diabetes"*, National Institutes of Health, 2016.

Gawande, Atul, *The Checklist Manifesto*, Picador, 2010.

Resources and Related Organizations

American Diabetes Association, www.diabetes.org, Email: AskADA@diabetes.otg, Phone: 1-800-342-2383.

American Podiatric Medical Association, www.apma.org, Email: AskAPMA@apma.org Phone: 1-800-8227

American Physical Therapy Association, www.apta.org, Email: consumer@apta.org

American Association of Diabetes Educators, www.diabeteseducator.org, Phone: 1-800-338-3633

Pedorthic Footwear Association, www.pedorthics.org, Email: info@pedorthics.org, Phone: 1-800-673-8447

About the Authors

Nicole Caviness, P.T. graduated as a physical therapist from Russell Sage College in 1996. She has over twenty years of experience as a physical therapist with an expertise in outpatient therapy. Nicole currently operates her own practice, Caviness Physical Therapy and Wellness, in Harrisburg, North Carolina.

Cherie Hardy, CDE is a Registered Nurse and board certified in Diabetes Education and Executive Nursing. She currently provides operational and clinical oversight to multiple diabetes education centers within a large medical organization in North Carolina.

Jeffrey Lehrman, DPM is in private practice in Fort Collins, Colorado, and was recently named one of "America's Most Influential Podiatrists." He is a Diplomate of the American Board of Foot and Ankle Surgery, a Fellow of the American Society of Podiatric Surgeons, a Certified Professional Coder, and a Master of the Professional Wound Care Association. Dr. Lehrman serves as an advisor to *WOUNDS* and *Podiatry Management* magazines and is an educator and consultant on topics such as coding, compliance, and wound care.

Kevin McDonald, DPM has over thirty years of experience in working on the feet of people with diabetes. He practices podiatry in Concord, North Carolina, and currently serves as President of InStride Foot and Ankle Specialists.

James Shipley, DPM practices podiatry with InStride Foot and Ankle Specialists in Mount Airy, North Carolina. He holds degrees from the University of North Carolina Chapel Hill, Temple University School of Podiatric Medicine, and Tulane University.

Thomas Verla, DPM earned his doctorate at Kent State University College of Podiatric Medicine and completed his surgical residency at the Hunter Holmes VA Hospital in Richmond. He then returned to the area he affectionately calls home in 2015 and practices podiatry in Spruce Pine, Boone, and Mars Hill, North Carolina. He is an avid outdoorsman and hunter. He and his wife, Laura, are expecting their first child in 2019.

Josh White, DPM is a podiatrist and certified Pedorthist who founded Safestep, a company focused on the proper fitting of diabetic footwear. He was recently named one of "America's Most Influential Podiatrists." Dr. White is a member of the National Coalition of Falls Risk and is a principal of the Healthy Outcomes EOS consulting firm.

CPSIA information can be obtained
at www.ICGtesting.com
Printed in the USA
FFHW011526160419
51799108-57189FF

9 780578 475486